Why Does It Float?

A **Just Ask** Book

Hi, my name is Christopher!

by Chris Arvetis
and Carole Palmer

illustrated by James Buckley

Copyright © 1983 by Rand McNally & Company
All rights reserved
Printed in the United States of America
by Rand McNally & Company

Library of Congress Catalog Card Number: 82-18526

First printing, 1983
Second printing, 1984

Rand McNally & Company
Chicago/New York/San Francisco

The little boat
floats too!

See the water line I drew. That shows how high the water is in the jar.

Put this boat
in the water.

When something
is put into water,
the water has to move
to make room for it.

No two things can
take up the same space
at the same time.
The water had to
rise higher to make
room for the boat.

We have to weigh
the water–
just the water that
was displaced.
That's the amount of
water above that line.

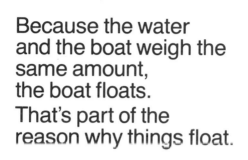
Because the water and the boat weigh the same amount, the boat floats. That's part of the reason why things float.

Let's do another experiment.
I'll put this block of wood in the water.

See this heavy
old piece of iron.
It sinks to
the bottom.

Let's change the shape
of the iron.
Let's make the iron
into the shape of a pan.

I can help.

Can I help?

When the iron was made
into a pan, its shape
was changed.
Now there's room for
air in the pan.
The pan covers a bigger
space in the water.
Its shape helps to
make it float.

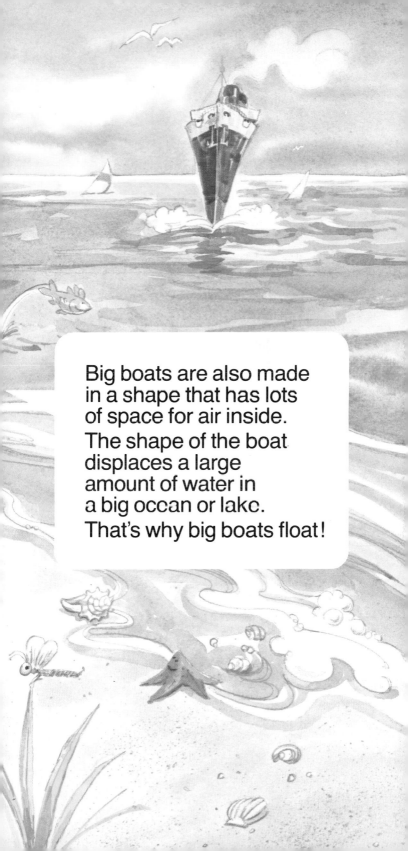

Big boats are also made
in a shape that has lots
of space for air inside.
The shape of the boat
displaces a large
amount of water in
a big ocean or lake.
That's why big boats float!